15
To His feet your trib - ute bring.
15
19
Ran - somed, healed, re - stored, for - giv - en,
19
23
Ev - er - more His prais - es sing.
23

27
Al - le - lu - ia! Al - le - lu - ia!
27
31
Praise the ev - er - last - ing King!
31
36
rit. and decresc.
36
rit. and decresc.

Slower and freely ♩ = ca. 88
39
mp
slight rit.
Fa - ther - like, He tends and spares us;
mp
39
mp Smoothly
slight rit.
43
a tempo
rit.
Well our fee - ble frame He knows.
43
a tempo
rit.
47
a tempo
slight rit.
In His hands He gent - ly bears us,
47
a tempo
Cued notes optional
slight rit.

51
a tempo
Res - cues us from all our foes.
51
a tempo
55
mf
(,)
sub. mp
slight rit.
Al - le - lu - ia! Al - le - lu - ia!
L.H.
59
a tempo
rit.
Wide - ly yet His mer - cy flows.

63
accel.
63
accel. and cresc.
Faster ♩ = ca. 112
67
Unison
f
Praise___ Him for His grace and fa - vor
Unison
f
67
Faster
f
Cued notes optional
(if tessitura is too high for alto and/or bass)
71
To___ our fa - thers in dis - tress;
71

75
Praise Him, still the same as ev - er,
79
Cued notes optional
Div.
cresc.
Glo - rious is His faith - ful - ness!
84
ff
An - gels in the height, a - dore Him;

88
You be - hold Him face to face.
88
92
Saints tri - um - phant bow be - fore Him;
92
96
Gath - ered in from ev - 'ry race.
96

100
(,)
Al - le - lu - ia! Al - le - lu - ia!
(,)
100
104
Praise with us the God of grace!
104
108
Al - le - lu - ia!
108
Sost. Ped.